# WEEKLY WR READER®
## EARLY LEARNING LIBRARY

## LIFE LONG AGO

# Ancient Egypt

by Tea Benduhn

Reading consultant: Susan Nations, M.Ed.,
author/literacy coach/consultant in literacy development

**Please visit our web site at: www.garethstevens.com**
**For a free color catalog describing Weekly Reader® Early Learning Library's list**
**of high-quality books, call 1-877-445-5824 (USA) or 1-800-387-3178 (Canada).**
**Weekly Reader® Early Learning Library's fax: (414) 336-0164.**

**Library of Congress Cataloging-in-Publication Data**

Benduhn, Tea.
    Ancient Egypt / by Tea Benduhn.
       p. cm. — (Life long ago)
    Includes bibliographical references and index.
    ISBN-13: 978-0-8368-7781-6 (lib. bdg.)
    ISBN-13: 978-0-8368-7786-1 (softcover)
    1. Egypt—Civilization—To 332 B.C.—Juvenile literature.
    2. Egypt—Social life and customs—To 332 B.C.—Juvenile literature. I. Title.
    DT61.B476   2007
    932—dc22                          2006030344

This edition first published in 2007 by
**Weekly Reader® Early Learning Library**
A Member of the WRC Media Family of Companies
330 West Olive Street, Suite 100
Milwaukee, WI 53212 USA

Managing editor: Valerie J. Weber
Art direction: Tammy West
Cover design, page layout, and illustrations: Dave Kowalski
Picture research: Diane Laska-Swanke

Picture credits: Cover, title, pp. 12, 14, 15 © Ronald Sheridan/Ancient Art & Architecture Collection; pp. 4, 5, 9, 16 © The Granger Collection, New York; pp. 6, 8, 18 Dave Kowalski/© Weekly Reader Early Learning Library; pp. 7, 13 © Werner Forman Archive; p. 10 © Richard T. Nowitz/CORBIS; p. 11 © Bruce Norman/Ancient Art & Architecture Collection; p. 17 © Gianni Dagli Orti/CORBIS; p. 19 © Stephen Coyne/Ancient Art & Architecture Collection; p. 20 © Mary Jelliffe/Ancient Art & Architecture Collection; p. 21 © Richard Ashworth/Ancient Art & Architecture Collection

Printed in the United States of America

1 2 3 4 5 6 7 8 9 10 10 09 08 07 06

# TABLE OF CONTENTS

**Cover and Title Page:** The ancient Egyptians carved a huge statue called the Sphinx.

# CHAPTER 1

## Where Did Mummies Come From?

Some scary movies show **mummies** coming back to life. Some show people looking for treasures in **pyramids**. Mummies and pyramids come from **ancient** Egypt. Do you know why the ancient Egyptians made mummies and pyramids?

Mummies were placed in painted wooden coffins. The colors on the coffin stayed bright for thousands of years.

Ancient Egyptians called their rulers **pharaohs**. When a pharaoh died, the Egyptians wrapped him in cloth. Making him into a mummy like this helped **preserve** his body. They put this mummy inside the pyramid. They filled the pyramid with many riches that they thought the pharaoh could use after death.

The ancient Egyptians used gold to cover their pharaohs' coffins. This coffin belongs to Pharaoh Tutankhamun, sometimes known as King Tut. He was just nine years old when he became ruler of ancient Egypt.

5

Egypt is a country in Africa. About five thousand years ago, most Egyptians lived near the Nile River. Every year, the Nile River flooded its banks. When the water left, the fertile soil it carried stayed behind. Crops for food grew easily in this soil.

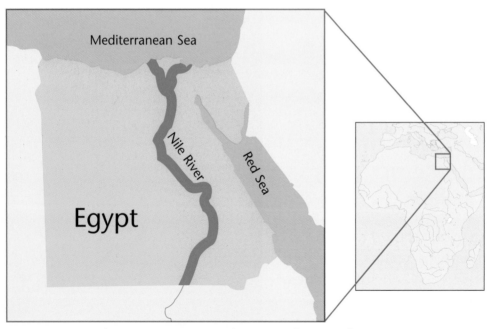

The green area on the map shows where ancient Egyptians lived along the Nile River.

Because farming was easy, the ancient Egyptians had time to do other things. They made pottery, wove cloth, and made jewelry. They built **temples** for their gods and decorated the walls with paintings. They also carved statues out of stone and developed a written language.

Ancient Egyptians also put artwork in wealthy peoples' **tombs.** Paintings on tomb walls showed what they thought would happen after death. This tomb's owner is shown kneeling to drink from a pool.

# 2

## What Did People Do in Ancient Egypt?

Pharoah

Priests

Overseers

Commanders and Scribes

Craftspeople and Farmers

Everyone reported to the pharaoh and followed his orders.

Ancient Egyptians thought the pharaoh was part god. Everyone worked for the pharaoh. He gave orders to priests, governors, and overseers. Royal overseers made sure the architects, army commanders, and law courts did their jobs right.

Most people were craftspeople or farmers. Some craftspeople made wooden boats, reed furniture, or mud-brick houses. Others made leather shoes, glass perfume jars, or stone statues of gods. Around their fields, farmers dug channels with gates that connected to the Nile River. They lifted the gates to water their crops.

The ancient Egyptians relied on the Nile River for farming. The Nile River runs along the bottom of this tomb painting. Channels flow from it.

Everything in the land belonged to the pharaoh, including all of the property, buildings, and crops. Everyone had to pay him taxes. They paid by giving him some of their crops, animals, or the items they made, such as pottery, baskets, or jewelry.

To show the pharaoh's importance, ancient Egyptians often painted the pharaoh larger than the people around him.

The base of the Great Pyramid at Giza covers 13 acres (5 hectares) of land.

Everyone helped build the pyramids. To build the Great Pyramid at Giza, four thousand stonemasons and one hundred thousand farmers worked three months each year for twenty years. Every day, they ate one hundred thousand bunches of onions and two hundred thousand loaves of bread.

A god with the head of a jackal, Anubis watched over the dead.

The ancient Egyptians buried the pharaoh's mummy in the pyramid. To make a mummy, ancient Egyptians removed the brain, heart, liver, intestines, lungs, and stomach. To dry out the body, they coated it in a type of salt called natron. After forty days, they rubbed the body in scented oils and wrapped it in linen bandages. Then they put the mummy inside a decorated coffin.

The ancient Egyptians prayed to many gods. The most important god was Ra, the Sun god. Many gods had the head of an animal. Horus's head was a falcon. Hathor had the head of a cow. She was the goddess of love and laughter.

A statue of the god Horus stands at the entrance to the Temple of Horus.

# CHAPTER 3

## What Was Life Like in Ancient Egypt?

If you lived in ancient Egypt, your family might live in a small house made of mud bricks. The doors and windows would be small to keep out heat from the Sun. Most homes had a flat roof. Stairs led to the roof so the family could sleep outside on hot nights.

This clay model shows what a typical house looked like in ancient Egypt.

For fun, families played a game called Senet. It was one of the first board games invented!

Fathers usually left for a few months out of the year to help build a pyramid for the pharaoh. Mothers looked after the children at home. Families were considered blessed if they had many children.

Most children did not go to school. Their parents usually taught them to do the same types of jobs they had, such as weaving cloth, making mud bricks, building furniture, or working with metal. By the time children were ten years old, they were ready to start work on their own. Girls could get married as young as twelve years old!

In this wall painting, a father teaches his son how to make bread in about 2400 B.C.

Scribes wrote important information in hieroglyphics.

Children of wealthy parents were able to attend school. They learned to read a special type of writing called **hieroglyphics**. They memorized more than seven hundred tiny pictures that stood for words and sounds. People who wrote hieroglyphics were called scribes.

# How Are We Like Ancient Egyptians Today?

Do you learn math in school?  So did the ancient Egyptians!  They needed math to build the pyramids. With math, the ancient Egyptians could measure huge blocks and make them the right size.  They could also count the right number of blocks to make the pyramid.

The Great Pyramid at Giza is 482 feet (147 meters) tall, 755 feet (230 m) wide, and contains 2.3 million blocks.

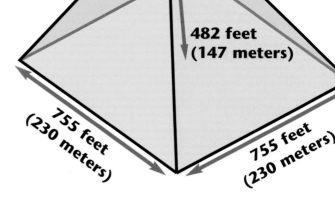

**482 feet (147 meters)**

**755 feet (230 meters)**

**755 feet (230 meters)**

Statues stand between the giant columns at the Luxor Temple in Karnak, Egypt.

Have you ever seen a building with big columns? Maybe your public library, local government building, or nearby university has columns. The ancient Egyptians were the first people to make columns for buildings.

When you write notes to your friends, do you ever use pictures, like a smiley face or star, instead of words? The ancient Egyptians wrote using images, too. The ancient Egyptians were one of the first **civilizations** to invent writing.

Ancient Egyptians used pictures of birds, people, and other items to stand for words.

What would writing be without paper? The Egyptians were the first to use a type of paper called **papyrus**. They made papyrus from reeds that grew along the banks of the Nile River. Without the Egyptians' invention of papyrus, there might not be any pages in this book!

As shown in this modern photograph, long strips of reeds are layered to make papyrus.

# GLOSSARY

**ancient** — old, from a very long time ago

**channels** — ditches in the ground for water to flow through

**civilizations** — groups of people living the same way of life as each other

**craftspeople** — people who made items for sale such as jewelry, furniture, boats, or pottery

**fertile** — able to grow a lot of plants

**hieroglyphics** — a type of writing that uses pictures to stand for sounds or words

**jackal** — a wild, doglike animal

**linen** — soft, light cloth made of flax threads, similar to cotton

**mummies** — prepared bodies wrapped in cloth for burial

**papyrus** — a type of paper made out of reeds

**preserve** — keep from rotting

**pyramids** — stone buildings with four triangular sides

**reed** — a strong, sturdy plant that grows along the banks of rivers

**stonemasons** — people who build with stones

**taxes** — payments to the government

**temples** — buildings for worship

**tombs** — buildings for burial

**university** — a college or school that people attend after finishing high school

# FOR MORE INFORMATION

## Books

*Ancient Egypt.* Curious Kids Guides (series). Philip Steele (Kingfisher)

*Egypt.* Scholastic History Readers (series). Stephen Krensky (Scholastic Paperbacks)

*Mummies and Pyramids.* Magic Tree House Research Guides (series). Will Osborne and Mary Pope Osborne (Turtleback Books)

*Valley of the Golden Mummies.* Smart about History (series). Joan Holub (Grosset & Dunlap)

## Web Site

### History for Kids: Ancient Egypt
*www.historyforkids.org/learn/egypt/index.htm*
Find out about the clothing ancient Egyptians wore, the games they played, and more.

# INDEX

## About the Author

Tea Benduhn writes and edits books for children and teens. Her book reviews, author interviews, and articles have appeared in magazines and newspapers. She lives in the beautiful state of Wisconsin.